WITHDRAWN

D1467467

OILS

Designed and produced by
Aladdin Books Ltd
70 Old Compton Street
London W1V 5PA

First published in the
United States in 1989 by
Gloucester Press
387 Park Avenue South
New York, NY 10016

ISBN 0 531 17136 1

Library of Congress Catalog
Card Number: 88 83106

Printed in Belgium

Author   Ian Mercer
            Geological Museum, London

Design   David West
            Children's Book Design

Editor   Scott Steedman

Researcher Cecilia Weston-Baker

Illustrator Louise Nevett

Consultant Dr. Keith Eastwood
            Geologist

CONTENTS

Photographic Credits:
Cover and pages 17 and
21: Aladdin Books; pages
4, 5 and 24: Robert
Harding; page 7: Science
Photo Library; page 8:
Australian Information
Service; pages 9 and 11:
Hutchison Library; page
13: Christine Osbourne;
page 14: Dr. G. T. Boalch;
page 22: Photosource;
page 23 (top): Zefa; page
23 (bottom): Vanessa
Bailey; page 25: Mike
Gethin/Defence
Magazine; page 30:
Wellcome Institute
Library, London.

RESOURCES TODAY

OILS

Ian Mercer

GLOUCESTER PRESS
New York · London · Toronto · Sydney

OILS AROUND US

We depend on oils for many different things. They are used in cooking and cleaning, to make paints and plastics, and to run cars and ships. There are many types of oils, and different oils are used in different ways. For example, we fry food in corn oil and lubricate engines with mineral oil. But all oils, whether they come from sunflowers, fish or from rocks beneath the Earth's surface, are made of substances which were once parts of living things.

Car fuel comes from petroleum, or mineral oil

There are three kinds of oils – vegetable oils, animal oils and mineral oils. All three are produced on an industrial scale. Some of the world's largest crops, like corn, cotton and soya, provide us with vegetable oils. We get animal oils from farm animals and fish. Mineral oil is called petroleum (Latin for rock-oil). Every day, millions of tons of this oil are pumped out of the ground. Whenever we fill our cars with fuel we are using mineral oil for energy.

The inset shows food frying in vegetable oil

OILS FROM PLANTS AND ANIMALS

The most common vegetable oils come from seeds, nuts and fruits – from sunflower seeds, peanuts and olives, for example. Animal oils come from layers of fat under the skin, or from organs like the liver. Many plants and animals are rich in oils and fats (fats are simply oils in a solid state). They use oils and fats as a way of storing energy.

We cannot live without oils and fats. Fats help to build parts of the body, such as the brain, nerves and the retina at the back of the eye. You need fat to make up the outer skin of every cell in your body. As our bodies use up oils and fats we must replace them in our diet.

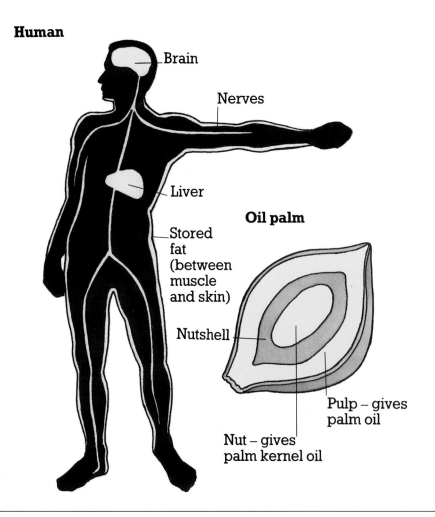

Human

- Brain
- Nerves
- Liver
- Stored fat (between muscle and skin)
- Nutshell

Oil palm

- Pulp – gives palm oil
- Nut – gives palm kernel oil

Oils and fats in animals . . . .
Oils and fats are high in food energy. Many animals, including humans, store fat under their skin. This fat provides good insulation against the cold. The brain and liver are both rich in fats.

. . . and plants
Plants fill their seeds, nuts or fruits with oils and fats. The fruit of the oil palm, grown in the tropics, is picked for its oil. Palm oil comes from the outer flesh of the fruit, while palm kernel oil comes from the inner "nut."

A close-up of human fat cells, taken with an electron microscope

GROWING AND HARVESTING

All over the world plants and animals are grown for the oils and fats they contain. Animals such as cows and goats are farmed for their milk, which is rich in fat. The milk is processed in a dairy, where some of it is made into butter and cheese. Other useful oils come from sheep, pigs, goats, and fish such as tuna. The oils are extracted from the fatty parts of these animals.

Vegetable oil crops are grown in huge groves and fields – in the United States, millions of acres of land are used for growing soy beans, sunflowers and corn. After harvesting, the seeds or fruit are transported by ship or train to special mills. Here the oils will be extracted.

Sheep are farmed for their wool and meat – and also for their oils

A sunflower field in France

EXTRACTING THE OIL

Getting oil out of plant and animal cells is called "extraction." Vegetable oils are extracted in oil mills. When the seeds or fruit arrive at the mill they are stored in huge silos. Then they are cleaned and the oils are extracted using pressure, heat or chemicals. Sometimes two or three of these processes are used one after the other, to extract as much oil as possible.

Animal oils are extracted by heating – fatty bits are boiled or steam-cooked and the oil is skimmed off. The fat extracted from cattle, sheep and goats is called tallow. Tallow is used to make soap and candles. Lard and lard oil, used in cooking and as lubricants, come from pig fat.

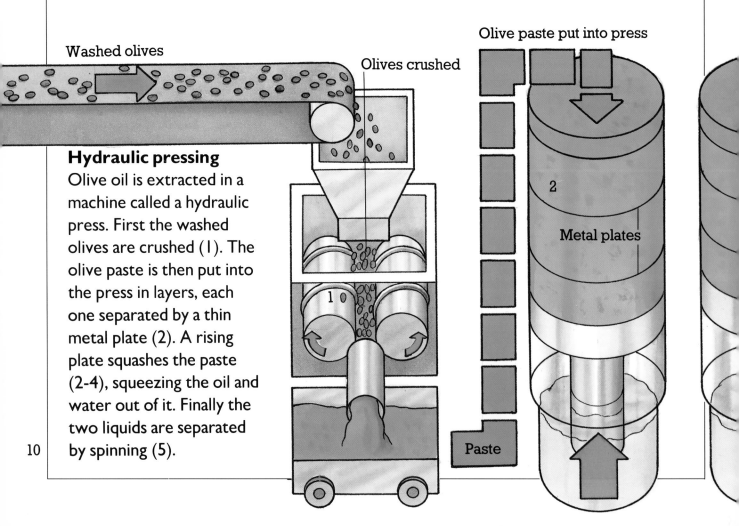

Washed olives

Olives crushed

Olive paste put into press

Hydraulic pressing
Olive oil is extracted in a machine called a hydraulic press. First the washed olives are crushed (1). The olive paste is then put into the press in layers, each one separated by a thin metal plate (2). A rising plate squashes the paste (2-4), squeezing the oil and water out of it. Finally the two liquids are separated by spinning (5).

Metal plates

Paste

10

Olive picking in Algeria

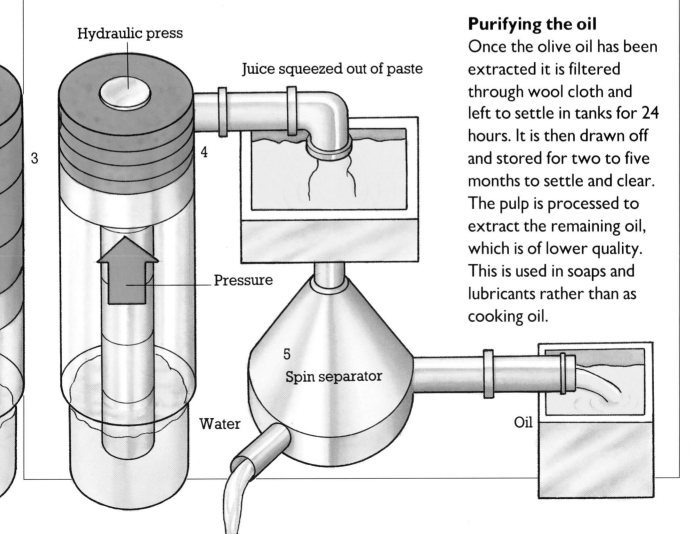

Hydraulic press

Juice squeezed out of paste

3

4

Pressure

5
Spin separator

Water

Oil

Purifying the oil

Once the olive oil has been extracted it is filtered through wool cloth and left to settle in tanks for 24 hours. It is then drawn off and stored for two to five months to settle and clear. The pulp is processed to extract the remaining oil, which is of lower quality. This is used in soaps and lubricants rather than as cooking oil.

SOLVENT EXTRACTION

Pressing does not remove all the oil from seeds and fruits. The remaining oil can be extracted with a solvent, a liquid which dissolves the oil. This process is called solvent extraction. First the solvent is poured over the vegetable pulp. The oil and the solvent are then separated by heating.

Some oils, such as soy bean oil, are only extracted by solvent. Soy beans contain less oil than peanuts or olives. Nevertheless the oil is easy to extract. This is because the beans can be rolled into thin flakes which are easily soaked by the solvent. Soy is the United States' largest crop, and the country produces enormous amounts of soy bean oil.

Extracting soy bean oil
Soy bean oil is extracted using a solvent made from petroleum. First the soy beans are cracked open, lightly heated and flaked. Then the flaked beans are fed into a moving chain of baskets while the solvent is poured over them. As the chain travels around, more solvent is poured over the beans until all the oil is dissolved. The flakes are then tipped out and replaced and the liquid is piped to the distiller. Here steam heat separates the oil from the solvent.

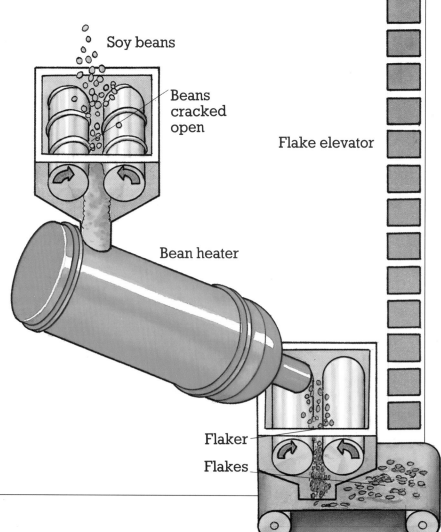

Soy beans

Beans cracked open

Flake elevator

Bean heater

Flaker

Flakes

12

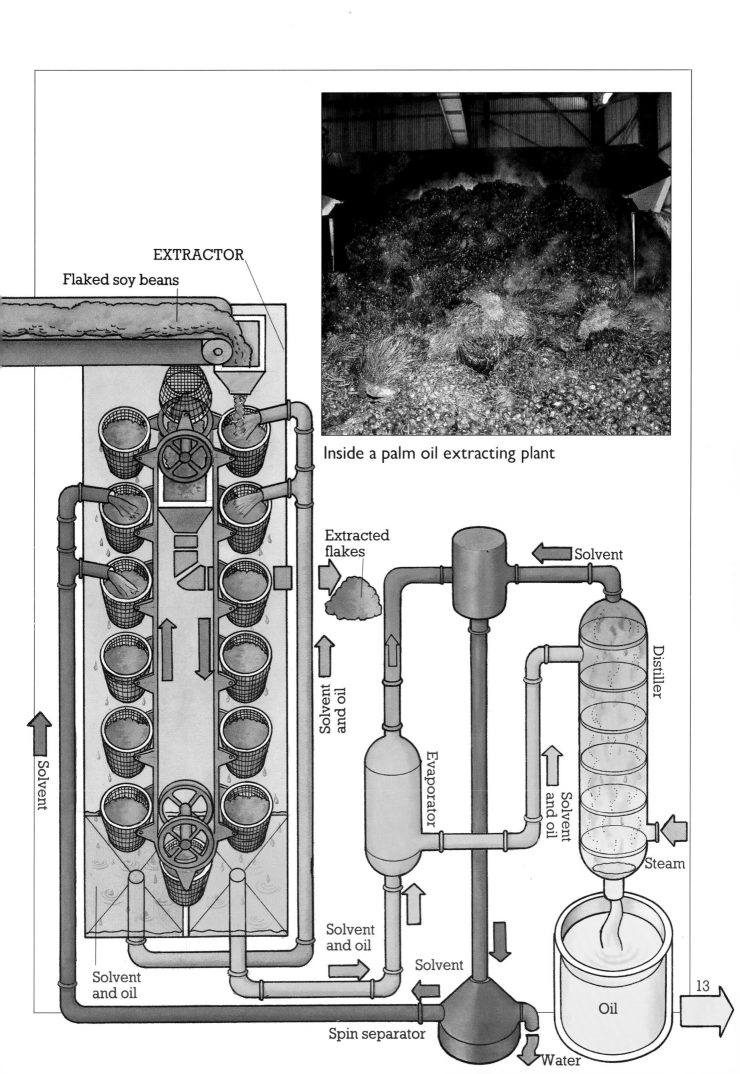

EXTRACTOR

Flaked soy beans

Inside a palm oil extracting plant

Extracted flakes

Solvent

Solvent and oil

Solvent

Solvent and oil

Solvent

Solvent and oil

Solvent and oil

Solvent and oil

Evaporator

Distiller

Steam

Spin separator

Oil

Water

HOW PETROLEUM IS FORMED

Mineral oil, or petroleum, is another sort of oil that comes from living things. But unlike animal and vegetable oil, petroleum takes many millions of years to form. It comes from the remains of tiny water plants and animals. They die and settle in the mud on the seabed. Gradually, more mud and sand pile up on top, burying the plant and animal remains. Over the years, intense heat turns the oily, fatty and waxy parts of the bodies into petroleum.

Natural gas, another substance which we use for energy, is often found with petroleum. It is formed deeper beneath the Earth's surface, where the heat of the rocks is even greater.

The photograph shows tiny plants found in plankton – the source of petroleum

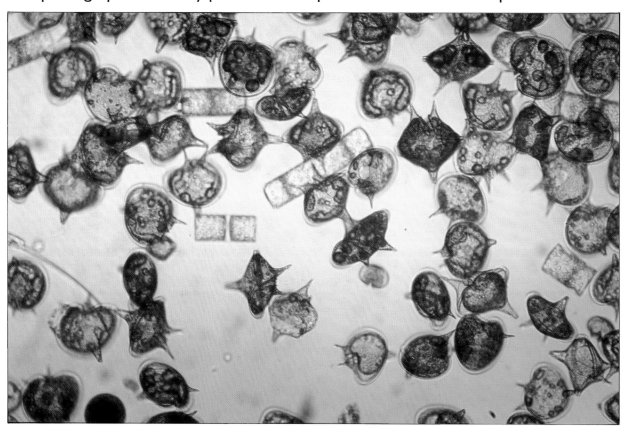

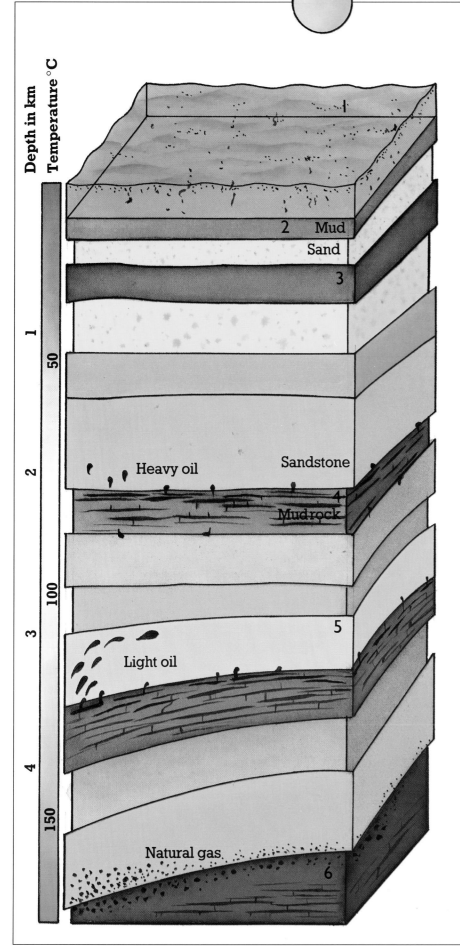

Depth in km Temperature °C

50

100

150

1

2

3

4

Mud

Sand

3

Heavy oil   Sandstone

4

Mudrock

5

Light oil

Natural gas

6

Oil and gas formation

1 Just beneath the surface of a lake or sea, tiny plants and animals – plankton – use sunlight energy to grow.

2 As the plankton dies, it settles on the seabed and decays in the stagnant mud. Some of its oily and waxy parts are preserved.

3 These change into dark brown specks in the hardened mud – the stored sunlight energy is buried deeper and deeper.

4 Where the mudrock is buried deeply it becomes hot. The specks in the rock begin to ooze with thick, heavy oil.

5 The deeper the rock is buried, the hotter it becomes, and the more oil is produced. When the rock becomes scalding hot it oozes with light, runny oil.

6 As the rock gets hotter still, the oil released becomes lighter and lighter. Eventually natural gas – mostly a gas called methane – is produced.

WHERE OIL AND GAS ARE FOUND

Oil and gas are valuable resources, and a lot of time and money is spent trying to find them. They are found trapped beneath the Earth's surface in areas called fields. To locate fields, special techniques such as echo-sounding are used. But the only way to make sure that oil is present is to drill a well.

How are fields formed? When oil and gas are created, they rise upward through the rock. Some reaches the surface and is lost. But some becomes trapped beneath a layer of impermeable (leakproof) rock – forming a field. The oil and gas are held in the cracks and pores of the rock below, like water in a sponge.

Finding and extracting oil and gas
Geologists search for likely areas where oil and gas may be hidden beneath the Earth's surface. They know the sort of rock formations which will trap oil and gas. Some traps are formed by domed-up rock layers (1). To find traps like these, sound waves are used in echo-sounding (2). The traps are then tested for oil or gas by drilling test wells – called wildcat wells – into them. To be worth extracting, there must be a lot of oil which flows easily from the rock.

When oil or gas are discovered far out at sea, production platforms may be built (3). These carry power plants, factories, drilling rigs and hotels for the workers. The oil and gas are extracted through wells at different angles. Water is often used to help force the oil out.

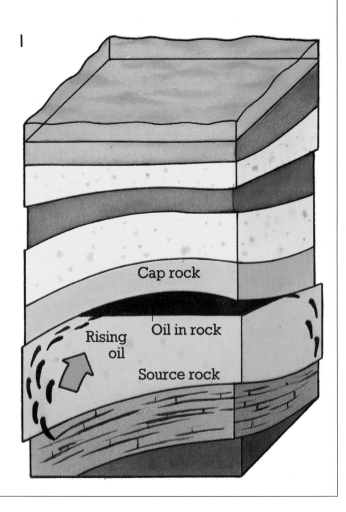

Cap rock

Rising oil

Oil in rock

Source rock

Drilling for oil on an exploration rig

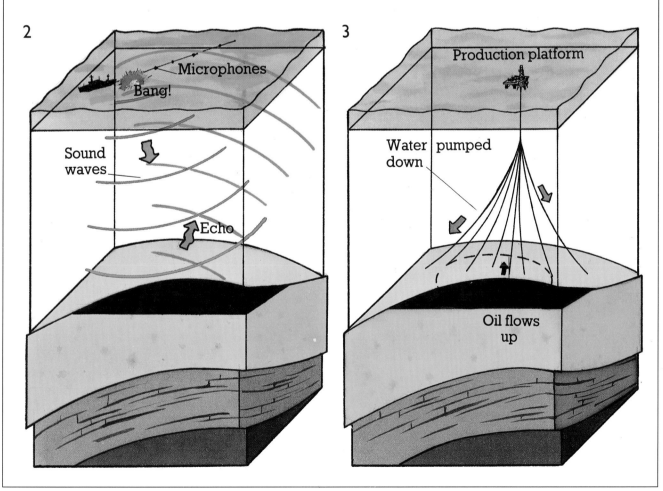

2
Microphones
Bang!
Sound waves
Echo

3
Production platform
Water pumped down
Oil flows up

OILS – A CLOSER LOOK

If we take a close look at the chemical structures of the different kinds of oils, we can see what they have in common. Like all substances, oils are made up of billions of tiny building blocks called atoms, which join together to form molecules. The molecules that make up different oils are all arranged in a similar way. They are made up of chains of carbon atoms which have hydrogen atoms attached to them.

Mineral oil (petroleum)
The molecules which make up this oil are called hydrocarbon molecules, because they are built of hydrogen and carbon atoms. The carbon atoms join up to make chains (right) and rings. Some chains are very long, but most are shorter than 20 carbon atoms. Natural gas has the shortest chains.

Animals/vegetable oils
These oils are also made of carbon and hydrogen, but they contain oxygen atoms as well. Each molecule is made of three carbon chains which are joined onto a substance called glycerine, which has atoms in an E-shape. The chains are usually 16 or more carbon atoms long.

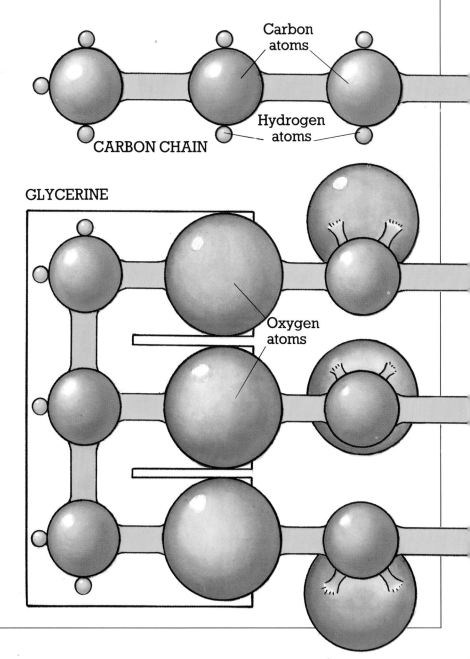

Carbon atoms

Hydrogen atoms

CARBON CHAIN

GLYCERINE

Oxygen atoms

Two fats we eat all the time are butter and margarine. They are made of millions of tiny water drops set in fat. Fats like these are solid because their carbon chains are stronger than those in oils. Oils, made from short and weak chains, are runny at room temperature.

Oils and fats feel greasy because their carbon chains slide past each other and make them slippery. Sweet-smelling plant oils called essential oils have different atomic patterns from the greasy oils.

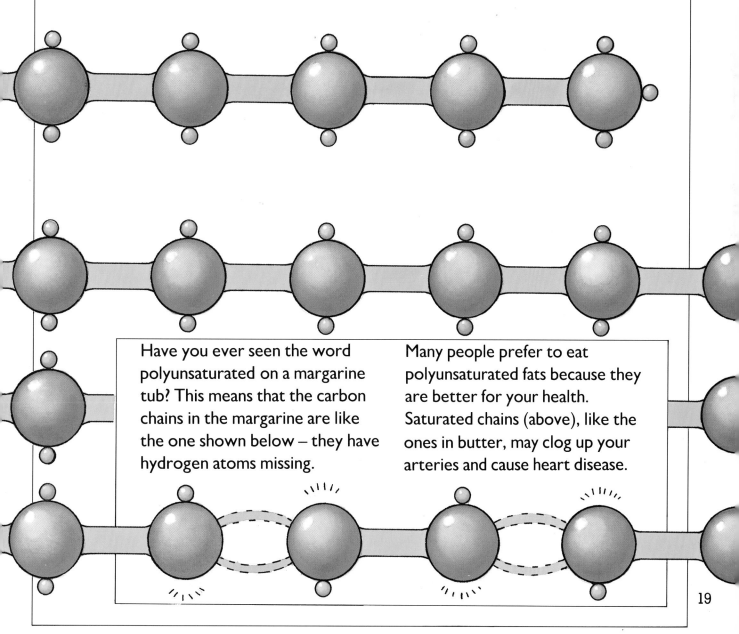

Have you ever seen the word polyunsaturated on a margarine tub? This means that the carbon chains in the margarine are like the one shown below – they have hydrogen atoms missing.

Many people prefer to eat polyunsaturated fats because they are better for your health. Saturated chains (above), like the ones in butter, may clog up your arteries and cause heart disease.

19

REFINING AND REMAKING

Most oils are filtered, purified or processed before they are used. Animal and vegetable oils are treated with chemicals to lighten their color. The mineral oil that comes out of the ground, crude oil, must first be separated from water and gas. The oil is then shipped or piped to a special factory called a refinery. There the oil is refined – purified and separated into different products, including gasoline and kerosene.

The carbon chains of many oils are altered, or remade, to produce more useful substances. For instance, hydrogen is removed from chains to create weak links. Oils with these weak links are more easily converted into products like plastics.

Adding hydrogen atoms
Oils can be converted into other useful products by adding hydrogen atoms to their carbon chains. For instance, margarine is made from vegetable oils and fish oils. Hydrogen is added to their weak, polyunsaturated chains of atoms. This hardens the oils to make fat. The hydrogen gas is mixed with hot oil under pressure. Just enough hydrogen is added to make fat that is soft enough to spread easily. If too much hydrogen is added, a hard fat like tallow can be made.

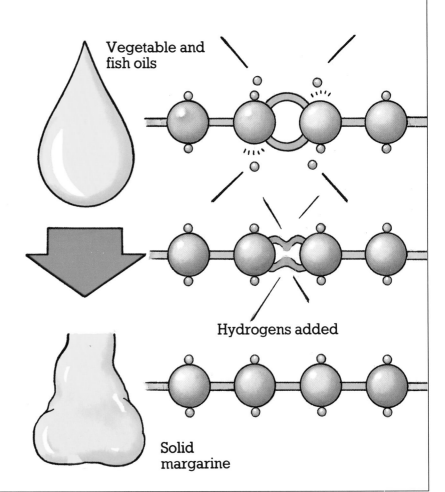

Vegetable and fish oils

Hydrogens added

Solid margarine

Cracking
Heavy oils from petroleum are broken down into lighter, more valuable oils by splitting their long carbon chains. This process is known as cracking. It takes place in special heaters called cat crackers.

Heat breaks carbon chains

Smaller chains produced

Mineral oil is processed in a refinery

OILS FOR KITCHENS AND CARS

In your home there are many foods and other products containing oils and fats. All sorts of chemicals come from oils, fats and natural gas, and many things around you are made from these chemicals. Listed below and opposite are some of the products made from oils and fats or which are made with their help.

When you are out shopping look at the labels on food packages to see what is in them. Look at all the different kinds of cooking oil. Sometimes the label will tell you where they are from, and what quality they are. Most plastics are made from petroleum – mineral oil – and natural gas. How many different kinds of plastic can you find?

Mineral oil (petroleum)
Petroleum is used to make paints (left). But its most important use is as a fuel. Various petroleum products, including diesel oil and kerosene, are burned as fuels and also used as grease and lubricants. Other products are processed to make plastics, which are made into a multitude of objects including curtains, dishes, clothing, even car bodies.

Petroleum products are also used in solvents, chemicals like dyes, medicines like aspirin, and in detergents.

Animal fats and oils

Oils from animals such as whales and cows are used in perfumes and cosmetics (left). However, most animal oils are used in food production – as canning oil, butter and butterfat, pet foods and shortening (including lard) for cooking and baking. Most soap is 75 to 80 percent tallow, which comes from the fat of farm animals. Animal oils are also used to make printing ink, glues, vitamins, shoe polish, medicines, candles, detergents, sealants and lubricants.

Vegetable oils and fats

Most vegetable oil is used as cooking and salad oil or as a raw material for making margarine (left). Drying oils such as linseed oil are used in putty, paints and varnish. Essential oils such as peppermint oil add flavor to candy and cakes and are used to make cosmetics, perfumes and medicines. Vegetable oils are also used to make soaps, plastics, chocolates, printing ink, resins, preservatives, candles, waterproofing, lubricating oil, polishes, car brake fluid and modeling clay.

OIL AND GAS FOR ENERGY

More than half the energy we use comes from mineral oil and natural gas. This energy is used in our homes, in industry and for transportation. There are more than 300 million vehicles in the world that run on oil. A jumbo jet uses 13,000 gallons of fuel to fly from New York to London.

Energy is released from oils by burning. This is true of all oils, whether they are used for energy in your body or in the cylinders of your car. Some petroleum is burned to generate electricity, which is safer and easier to transport. However, the way we burn petroleum is inefficient – our cars, planes and power stations lose a lot of energy as waste heat.

A power station where petroleum is burned to generate electricity

This jet fighter runs on highly-refined petroleum

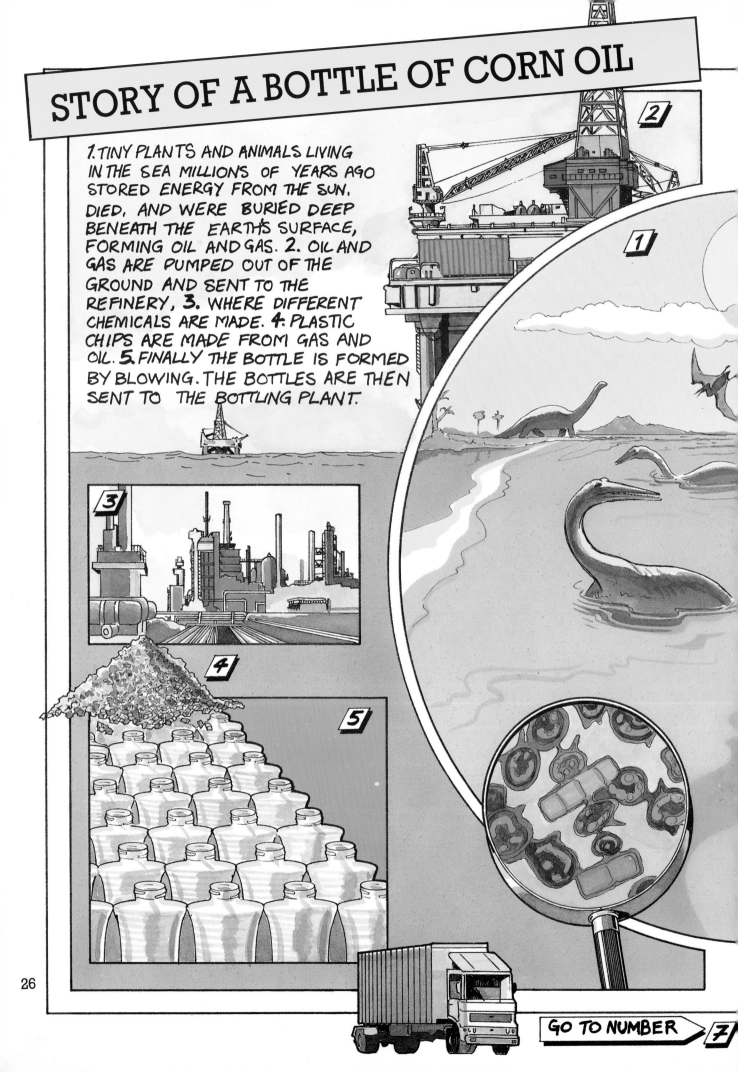

STORY OF A BOTTLE OF CORN OIL

1. TINY PLANTS AND ANIMALS LIVING IN THE SEA MILLIONS OF YEARS AGO STORED ENERGY FROM THE SUN, DIED, AND WERE BURIED DEEP BENEATH THE EARTH'S SURFACE, FORMING OIL AND GAS. 2. OIL AND GAS ARE PUMPED OUT OF THE GROUND AND SENT TO THE REFINERY, 3. WHERE DIFFERENT CHEMICALS ARE MADE. 4. PLASTIC CHIPS ARE MADE FROM GAS AND OIL. 5. FINALLY THE BOTTLE IS FORMED BY BLOWING. THE BOTTLES ARE THEN SENT TO THE BOTTLING PLANT.

26

GO TO NUMBER 7

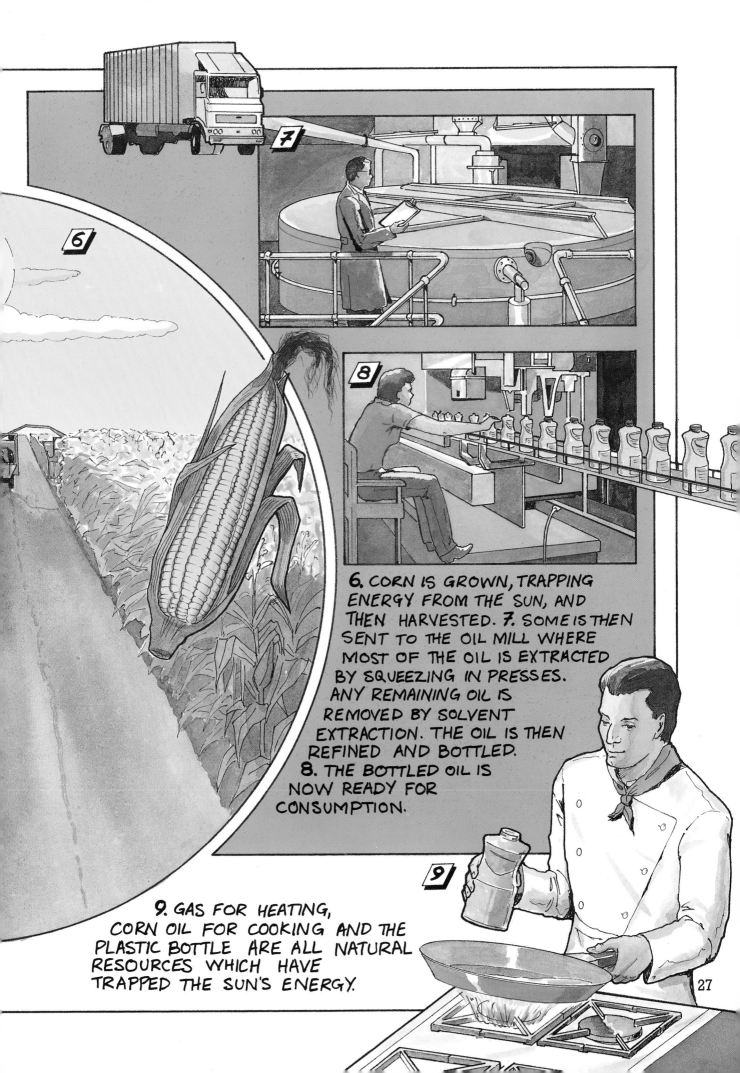

6. CORN IS GROWN, TRAPPING ENERGY FROM THE SUN, AND THEN HARVESTED. 7. SOME IS THEN SENT TO THE OIL MILL WHERE MOST OF THE OIL IS EXTRACTED BY SQUEEZING IN PRESSES. ANY REMAINING OIL IS REMOVED BY SOLVENT EXTRACTION. THE OIL IS THEN REFINED AND BOTTLED.
8. THE BOTTLED OIL IS NOW READY FOR CONSUMPTION.

9. GAS FOR HEATING, CORN OIL FOR COOKING AND THE PLASTIC BOTTLE ARE ALL NATURAL RESOURCES WHICH HAVE TRAPPED THE SUN'S ENERGY.

27

FACT FILE 1

Mineral oil – today and tomorrow

The map on the right shows where mineral oil and natural gas are produced in the world today. The light blue areas are continental shelves, shallow parts of the seas where much oil and gas has been found in the last 20 years.

More than half the world's proven oil reserves of 700,000 million barrels are in the Middle East. World production (below) is removing the more easily reached reserves at a great rate. More oil and gas will be found, but a lot of it will be in small fields or remote regions and will be difficult to produce. There may come a time when the Middle East will have the world's only oil that is cheap enough to produce. By this time, oil will probably be rising rapidly in price. Oil and gas will never run out – they will simply become too expensive to burn. Hopefully, research into other sources of energy and materials will provide us with alternatives to oil and gas before this happens. Meanwhile we must find ways of saving energy.

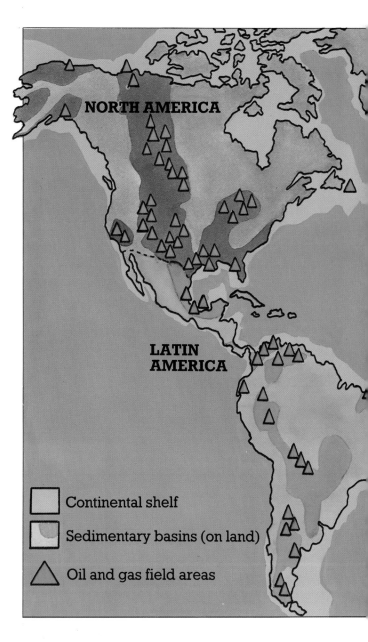

Continental shelf

Sedimentary basins (on land)

Oil and gas field areas

World Production of Petroleum

WESTERN EUROPE	4,018,000
MIDDLE EAST	12,867,000
AFRICA	5,059,000
NORTH AMERICA	11,436,000
LATIN AMERICA	6,649,000
ASIA AND AUSTRALIA	3,425,000
SOVIET UNION AND CHINA	15,265,000

WORLD TOTAL 58,719,000   Figures in barrels per day (one barrel = 159 liters)

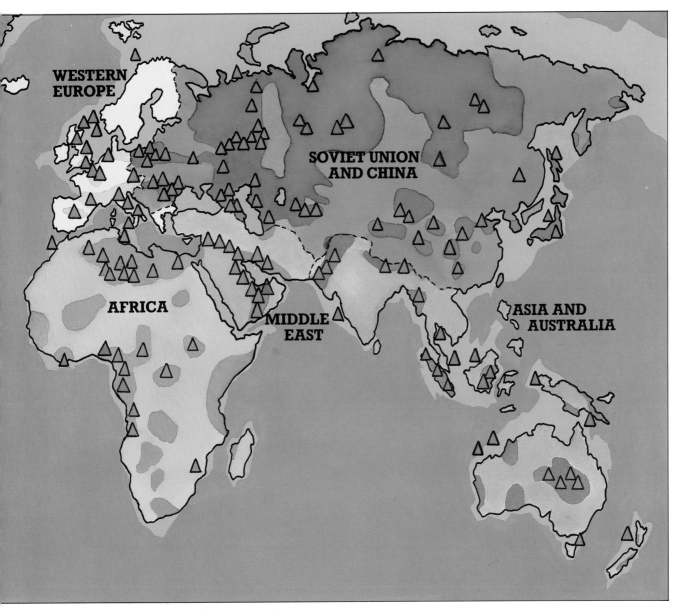

WESTERN
EUROPE

SOVIET UNION
AND CHINA

AFRICA

MIDDLE
EAST

ASIA AND
AUSTRALIA

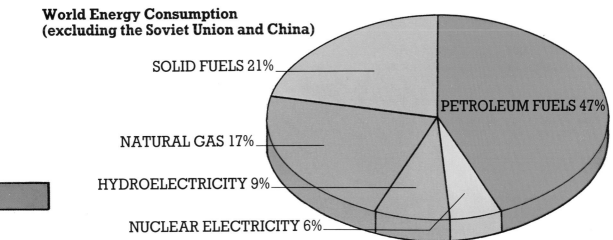

**World Energy Consumption
(excluding the Soviet Union and China)**

SOLID FUELS 21%

PETROLEUM FUELS 47%

NATURAL GAS 17%

HYDROELECTRICITY 9%

NUCLEAR ELECTRICITY 6%

FACT FILE 2

Animal and vegetable oils

Oil appears in the earliest known writing dealing with medical matters. A clay tablet 4,000 years old lists a remedy, and its ingredients include "tree oil." The oil was used by the *Asu* or doctor-priests of Mesopotamia (now Iraq). Hollow stones were used as oil lamps in caves in France more than 15,000 years ago. They were used in the Shetland Islands only 100 years ago. The lamp oil industry was based on colza, or rapeseed oil, until the start of the petroleum industry in the 1860s. Then crude oil was refined for use in lamps.

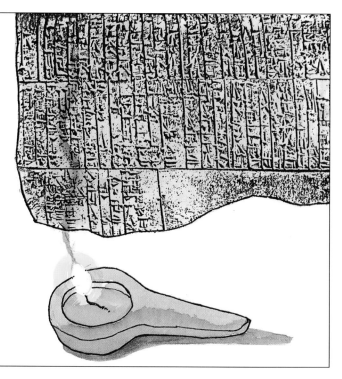

This diagram shows some of the plants and animals that provide us with oils

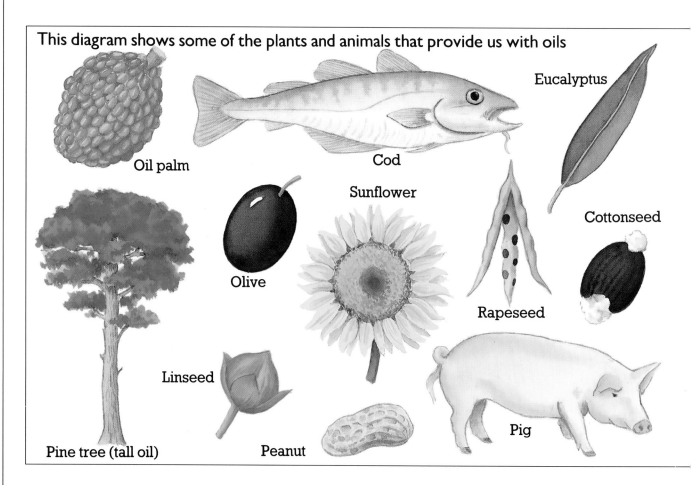

Oil palm

Cod

Eucalyptus

Olive

Sunflower

Cottonseed

Rapeseed

Linseed

Pig

Pine tree (tall oil)

Peanut

This map shows where three major vegetable oils are produced. Soybeans provide one-fifth of the world's vegetable oil. Soy oil is used in cooking, in industry and to make margarine. Olive oil and palm oil are both popular cooking oils. Other important oils include flax, sunflower, rapeseed and mustard oils. About 150 kinds of plants are also grown for essential oils.

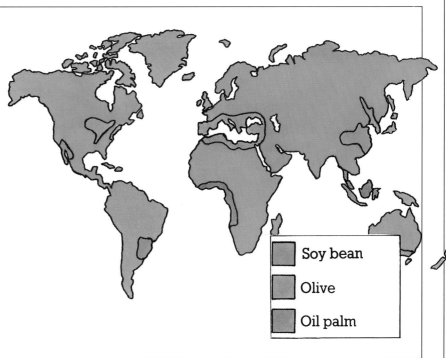

Soy bean

Olive

Oil palm

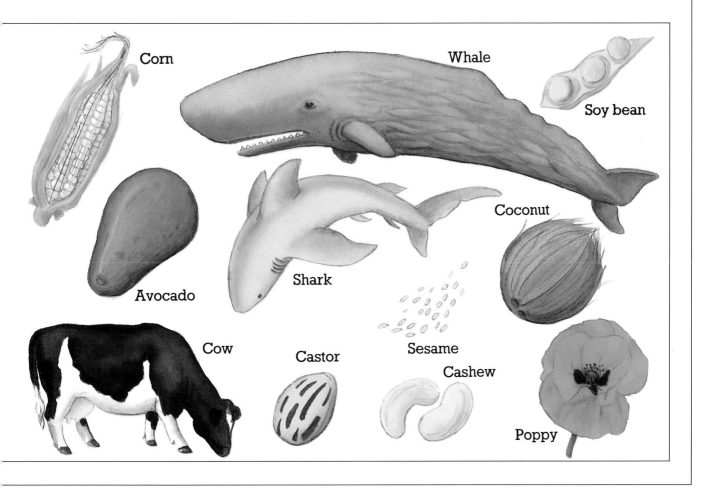

Corn

Whale

Soy bean

Avocado

Shark

Coconut

Cow

Castor

Sesame

Cashew

Poppy

31

GLOSSARY

Cracking
The process of breaking and re-shaping oil molecules by heating them.

Crude Oil
Mineral oil – petroleum – as it comes out of the ground. Crude oil is transported in pipelines or tankers.

Extraction
The process of getting oils out of rocks, animal cells or plant cells.

Field
An area where petroleum (and/or natural gas) has collected in rock layers beneath the surface of the Earth.

Hydrocarbon
A substance made of linked hydrogen and carbon atoms. Petroleum and natural gas are hydrocarbons.

Petroleum
Mineral oil, found in layers of rock beneath the Earth's surface.

Solvent
A substance, usually a liquid, that is able to dissolve another substance.

Tallow
Animal fat which comes from cattle, sheep and goats. Tallow is used to make soap and candles.

INDEX